Go to Heaven

Raymond Fell

PublishAmerica
Baltimore

First printing

ISBN: 1-4137-7553-5
PUBLISHED BY PUBLISHAMERICA, LLLP
www.publishamerica.com
Baltimore

Printed in the United States of America

Dedication

This book is being dedicated to all the brave men and women who have been killed or wounded while serving in the Armed Forces of the United States of America, especially in Iraq and Afghanistan.

As for those who were killed, they have gone to meet their All Loving God and let us all hope and pray that by sacrificing their lives, as they heroically did, they will gain their eternal reward in heaven.

To those who have been wounded, let us all hope and pray that they will be restored to good health and that their injuries and sufferings will deservedly earn them a place in the glorious kingdom of heaven for all eternity.

Thank you Geraldine
for all your editorial
assistance. God bless
you!

Ray

Table of Contents

Introduction

We have all heard that other expression, *"Go to ****!"* but this book has a more positive command. It attempts to describe in human terms what heaven might be like, but it also covers areas such as circumstances that could keep us out of heaven as well as topics that are important to reflect on as we make our way along our earthly path toward our heavenly goal.

Since our minds are finite, we really cannot think in terms of the infinite. It is just impossible to construct in our minds or thoughts what God or heaven must be like.

We read in the Bible that "eye has not seen, nor ear heard, the wonderful things that God has prepared for those who love Him." In fact, there are many passages in the Bible where we find Jesus talking about how we can be saved and possess everlasting life. So, there is no doubt about it, Jesus wants us all there.

CHAPTER ONE

A Reflection on God and Heaven

Before we can dwell on what it might be like in heaven, we need to reflect on our All Loving God. Many of us have been taught that God is omnipotent, meaning He is all powerful. It is just humanly impossible for us to comprehend how He could create a universe that has so much order in it. If He can do that for us, imagine what else He could do!

Even man, whom He created, has developed and invented things that are truly remarkable. There are so many things brought on by man's ingenuity at which most of us can only marvel. Look at the advancements in medicine, airplanes, space exploration, computers, etc. that have taken place just in the past century. If God can create human beings capable of such extraordinary accomplishments, what must He be like? Wouldn't you like to meet Him?

Many of us have been taught that God is omniscient, which means He knows everything about us, our innermost thoughts and desires; and there are billions of us. We can only wonder how could that be possible?

Many of us have learned from tradition and the Bible that God sent His only Son down to earth to redeem us from our sins by dying on the cross. God did this because He loves us.

God wants us to be with Him in heaven for all eternity but, having given us free will, God knows that some people will choose a path that will lead them away from Him, while others strive to follow His commandments.

If we dwell on what heaven might be like, even though our finite minds would not be close to guessing, this might cause us to think about heaven more than we do now. Some of us may not have given much thought about heaven, particularly with the many things going on in our busy lives. Should we be too busy to think of our life after this one? Don't forget, we'll be there for all eternity and our time on earth is miniscule compared to that! If we spend more time reflecting on heaven, we might make some changes in our lives that will direct us on the right path to get there.

When we get to heaven, can you imagine the people with whom we will want to meet? There may be famous people whom we have read about in history books, people who lived before Christ, not to mention members of our family, relatives and friends. Many of us would be thrilled to converse with Abraham Lincoln, George Washington, Thomas Edison; the list is endless.

Of course, the first One we will meet is our All Loving God. Can you just picture the scene when we come face-to-face with Him? What will He say to us? What will we say to Him? If we have talked to Him regularly while on earth, that meeting should be a joyful experience.

CHAPTER TWO

A Comparison Between Heaven and Earth

There is much evil in our world; some people have a great deal of anger and hatred in their hearts; some are greedy, jealous, lustful, selfish, dishonest, reckless, etc. We hear about aids epidemics, war rumors, starving children, rampant poverty in some countries, drug overdoses, homelessness, suicidal bombings, terrorist attacks, etc.

There will be NONE of this in heaven!

It is hard for us to imagine what our world would be like if we had peace throughout the world and everyone loved one another. We can be quite certain that this will never happen in our earthly dwelling place, but heaven is another story!

Let us reflect on things we deal with on earth that will be nonexistent in heaven. Time would not be a factor since heaven will be forever. What a treat that will be especially for people who say there isn't enough time in the day for what they want to do! There will be no need for clocks or watches. What a switch that will be for those whose lives revolve around the time of day!

We will not get tired or feel the need to sleep. Our bodies will not feel hunger, so it will not be necessary to eat. Sickness will be a thing of the past, as will pain and suffering. We will never feel sad or depressed, never shed tears, never experience disappointment, never be afraid; the list is endless!

We will not have to work for a living. That will please many who hate their jobs or can not get along with their bosses.

There will not be a need for money. What a blessing that will be for those who struggled all their lives trying to make ends meet!

Cars will be nonexistent, so we won't have to worry about traffic tie-ups, accidents, insurance, repairs, gas prices, tailgaters, registration, icy roads, etc. Feel free to add to this list.

Imagine a place without storms, hurricanes, earthquakes, terrorist attacks, nuclear war threats, etc.; a place where peace is the order of the day!

There would be no need for policemen, soldiers, homeland security, hidden cameras, privacy acts, lawyers and courts of law.

We would see no one suffering with afflictions, addictions, cancer, Alzheimers disease, malnutrition, aids, heart disease; this list could go on and on.

Travel will be wherever we wish to go with no restrictions. If we are in heaven while earth still exists, since our glorified bodies will be invisible to the human eye, we will be able to go wherever we wish on earth. In other words, we will be able to do things that as earthlings we could not do. If we want to sit on the field while the Super Bowl is being played, we could do it and not even be noticed. We might want to ride on the shoulders of a marathoner as he runs the twenty-six miles. We would have no limits or barriers as we do now.

We might want to fly around the universe and explore God's whole creation and visit constellations that man has not discovered. For all we know, there could be other planets on which people live.

No one really knows what we will do in heaven, but just to be in the presence of Almighty God in all His splendor might be all we would want or need.

It is difficult for us to imagine what it must be like to be completely happy and satisfied all the time. There will be no disagreements, arguments, shouting, temper tantrums, dishonesty, lying, stealing, killing, child abuse, rape, etc., etc. How long could you make this list?

We won't need houses to live in, so all those chores around the house will be passé. There will be no grass to cut, no heating bills, no roofs to repair, no appliances to break down; life definitely will not be the same!

In life there are things people really enjoy doing, no doubt about it. Skiing, swimming, horseback riding, sailing, running, bowling, golfing, etc. are all fun things in which people find pleasure. "I'd rather be fishing," is a commonly seen bumper sticker.

The next time you sit down and enjoy a delicious meal, try to imagine whatever awaits us in heaven will greatly surpass that earthly pleasure. It is not easy to use the imagination on things we cannot envision and of which we have no knowledge.

What we find pleasurable here on earth is often interrupted by reality. Our vacation that has been planned all year must come to an end! The new car that we just bought is spending undue time in the dealer repair shop! Our favorite team is doing poorly! Poor weather may cause our plans to be cancelled! Pleasure on earth is fleeting, but in heaven it will never end. That is a difficult phenomenon for us to grasp. Keep in mind the pleasure that we will experience in heaven is not known to us and we won't know until we get there.

Our clothing is another aspect of life that needs to be addressed. Imagine not worrying about what we are going to wear! We have no idea what our glorified bodies will be like in heaven. Maybe we all will wear white robes!

Our knowledge is very limited in our present existence as humans. What we have learned from our reading and formal schooling is almost surface knowledge compared to all the information that is found in all kinds of books. For instance, in any given library there are thousands of books written by thousands of authors. It would be impossible to have the time to read all those books and, of course, many of them would be of little interest to us. Then there is the question of remembering all that we have read.

When we get to heaven we will find out the answers to questions that puzzled us on earth. We will know what caused so many people to have cancer. We will discover exactly what happened with Adam and Eve in the Garden of Eden. We will know the truth about all the controversial subjects that divided so many people over the centuries. For example, the controversy over the Shroud of Turin (the cloth that displays the image of Jesus as He lay in the tomb) will be resolved. We will have revealed to us just how accurate our history books were. We will discover exactly how God created the universe. He may even show us how He did it! Anything we want to know will be accessible information instantaneously. Reading will not be necessary because our glorified bodies will have minds that will automatically absorb whatever we wish to know.

Our ability to communicate with others will also be automatic. There will be no such thing as a language barrier as we know it on earth. Our hearing and vision will also be far superior to what we have now.

Most of us enjoy listening to great performers in the music field, whether they sing or play an instrument. We also appreciate watching great athletes in action, listening to great speakers make their presentations, viewing famous works of art; just to name a few things in which we find enjoyment.

In heaven, we will be able to not only duplicate these great performers and artists but will even surpass whatever abilities they had on earth as humans.

Imagine being able to sing better than Frank Sinatra or some of the great opera stars! Could you see yourself as a better artist than Michelangelo?

This brings us back to what we will do in heaven. Will we sing, paint, play games, or other such things, or will we be doing things that mere humans could never imagine?

If earth is still in existence after we go to heaven, who knows what we will be able to do. We might spend time (which will be nonexistent for us) watching over members of our family, guiding them by special powers that we may possess. Our loved ones in heaven may be watching over us right now as we live our daily lives.

It goes without saying that since no one has come back from heaven to tell us what it is like we can fantasize to our hearts content what it could be like there. The author of this book is doing that very thing as you read along. Who can disprove it? You can construct your own vision of what heaven will be like and use that as a motivational tool to gain heaven. You might be able to come up with ideas about heaven that will appeal to you better than this author has offered. The more time you spend reflecting on heaven, the greater the chances will be for you to direct your life toward that goal.

One of this author's favorite Bible stories about heaven is found in Luke 16:19-31.

It is as follows:

Once there was a rich man who dressed in purple and linen and feasted splendidly every day. At his gate lay a beggar named Lazarus who was covered with sores. Lazarus longed to eat the scraps that fell from the rich man's table. The dogs even came and licked his sores. Eventually, the beggar died. He was carried by angels to the bosom of Abraham. The rich man likewise died and was buried. From the abode of the dead where he was in torment, he raised his eyes and saw Abraham afar off, and Lazarus resting in his bosom.

"He called out, "Father Abraham, have pity on me. Send Lazarus to dip the tip of his finger in water to refresh my tongue, for I am tortured in these flames."

"My child," replied Abraham, "Remember that you were well off in your lifetime, while Lazarus was in misery. Now he has found consolation here, but you have found torment. And that is not all. Between you and us there is fixed a great abyss, so that those who might wish to cross from here to you cannot do so, nor can anyone cross from your side to us.

"Father, I ask you then," the rich man said, "send him to my father's house where I have five brothers. Let him be a warning to them, so that they may not end in this place of torment.

Abraham answered, "They have Moses and the prophets. Let them hear them."

"No, Father Abraham," replied the rich man. "But if someone would only go to them from the dead, then they would repent.

Abraham said to him, "If they do not listen to Moses and the prophets, they will not be convinced even if one should rise from the dead."

We need to have faith in order to believe in what comes after death. Jesus promised us eternal life if we believe in Him. What if He had not made any such promise? What if heaven did not exist? Life on earth would have no meaning. How empty life would be! It is safe to say there would be nothing but chaos in our lives and in our world. Let us rejoice that Jesus did promise us heaven and it is up to us to remove any obstacles that would get in our way of obtaining that goal.

CHAPTER THREE

Faith in God

Faith in God is so important in our lives as we strive toward our eternal reward in heaven. We have to believe that what we read in the Bible is the truly inspired word of God. Unfortunately, some people never read the Bible, seldom or never go to a church or place of worship, seldom or never pray, seldom or never give any thought to God's existence, and thus they have little or no faith.

There are others who believe that there is a God but do not go much further than that. Some people have lost their faith due to a variety of reasons. They may have been disillusioned by the bad actions of others, particularly by those who regularly attend church. Sexual abuse by priests has caused some Catholics to stop attending church services.

Faith in God can be lessened or lost by one's own sinful behavior. Whatever the case may be, faith can be restored by turning back to God. Prayer and good works can go a long way in strengthening one's faith.

Some people may claim they have lost their faith in God, but on the other hand, they can be very trusting. Most of us trust, or have confidence, in what takes place in our daily lives.

Parents trust that their children will be honest with them, and children trust that their parents will provide for them. When sick, we trust our doctors will make us better. When our cars malfunction, we trust our mechanics will repair them properly. We trust that our schools will provide a good education for our children.

We could worry ourselves to death about all kinds of circumstances, but most of us go about our lives trusting that nothing bad will happen to us. There are plenty of things we could worry about. We could worry about our house catching on fire, the airplane we are in crashing, our car losing its brakes going down a steep hill; the scenarios are countless. Fortunately, most of us are not worry warts. We just trust that we are safe and will continue to be safe. Naturally, we have to be safety conscious.

Some of us are more fortunate than others, but some people have experienced real tragedies in their lives, and we read about them all the time in the newspaper or see them on the television news.

The point being made here is that even though we know that tragedies occur with other people, we do not anticipate to be involved in any because we are, by nature, trusting.

So, if most of us are very trusting, it is conceivable that most of us have a strong faith. But as we can lose our trust and our confidence, we can also lose our faith.

Once again, in order to prevent our faith in God from weakening, we need to continue to pray and do good works.

CHAPTER FOUR

Church Attendance

Only thirty percent of Catholics attend church regularly according to church attendance records as well as other studies. Some Catholics stopped going to church after the scandal of sex abuse by priests was exposed. This was a sad chapter in the history of the Catholic Church, and it may take a long time for some Catholics to return to the fold.

Credit must be given to those who remained faithful to their church even though they were embarrassed and saddened by all the terrible stories they heard and read about.

It has been a very difficult time for priests who were innocent of any of these transgressions, but who had to continue their ministry knowing some people were looking at them suspiciously, wondering if they were also guilty of sexual abuse.

No matter what religion one professes, church attendance is important. When we are in a holy place of worship, we cannot help but think of God. The prayers we say, the hymns we sing and our very presence all give praise to God and strengthen us spiritually.

Hopefully, when we leave a church or synagogue, we take away something that will aid us to become better people. If we can improve our lives by regular church attendance, we might be able to influence others to do the same.

There are many reasons why some people do not go to church. If parents never bring their children to church, then these children may never go when they are parents and the cycle just extends itself. Some young adults might have gone to church when they were children, but lost interest as they got older. We sometimes hear about bad experiences people had with their pastor that caused them to stop attending church services. There are many Catholics who do not agree with some of the teachings of the church and, as a result, they join a different religion or give up on religion altogether. There are cases where a practicing Catholic marries a non-Catholic who doesn't attend church and ends up not going either.

The author of this book, who is a practicing Catholic, believes that most people of all religions and faiths are going to be saved. Unfortunately, if people don't attend church or synagogue regularly, it prevents them from establishing a close relationship with God, which will be further covered in a subsequent chapter.

Attending church shows God that we love Him and want to know more about Him. No doubt He is pleased with those of us who go to church, and He would be delighted to have us encourage others who do not go, to do so.

Most of us are familiar with the Bible stories of the prodigal son and the lost sheep and the happiness that ensued upon their return. These stories definitely relate to those people who do not attend religious services or have no religious affiliation with God.

The stories can be found in the Bible in chapter 15 of St. Luke:

> Jesus said to them: "A man had two sons. The younger of them said to his father, 'Father, give me the share of the estate that is coming to me.' So the father divided up the property. Some days later, this younger son collected all his belongings and went off to a distant land where he squandered his money on dissolute living. After he had spent everything, a great famine broke out in that country and he was in dire need. So he attached himself to one of the propertied class of the place, who sent him to his farm to take care of the pigs. He longed to fill his belly with the husks that were fodder for the pigs, but no one made a move to give him anything. Coming to his senses, at last, he said: 'How many hired hands at my father's place have more than enough to eat, while here I am starving! I will break away and return to my father, and say to him, Father, I have sinned against God and you. I no longer deserve to be called your son. Treat me like one of your hired hands.' With that he set off for his father's house. While he was still a long way off, his father caught sight of him and was deeply moved. He ran out to meet him, threw his arms around his neck and kissed him. The son said to him, "Father, I have sinned against God and you; I no longer deserve to be called your son.

"The father said to his servants: 'Quick! Bring out the finest robe; put a ring on his finger and shoes on his feet. Take the fatted calf and kill it. Let us eat and celebrate because this son of mine was dead and has come back to life. He was lost and is found.' Then the celebration began."

Jesus told this parable:

"Who among you if he has a hundred sheep and loses one of them does not leave the ninety-nine in the wasteland and follow the lost one until he finds it? And when he finds it, he puts it on his shoulders in jubilation. Once arrived home, he invites friends and neighbors in and says to them, 'Rejoice with me because I have found my lost sheep.' I tell you, there will likewise be more joy in heaven over one repentant sinner than over ninety-nine righteous people who have no need to repent."

CHAPTER FIVE

Materialism

There is such an emphasis on materialistic things today that any thought of heaven is far removed from the minds of many people.

Television commercials bombard us continuously with messages and pictures that try to convince us of things we need or desire. Advertisements in magazines and newspapers are used for the same purpose. Retail stores make their wares very appealing as we walk through the aisles.

Credit cards are so accessible, and available credit is set to limits of $10,000 to $30,000 for many consumers. The minimum payments required are so low and appealing that the unwary user may not even realize how many years it would take to pay off the entire balance.

Many people are so preoccupied with having materialistic things that they are blinded from any visions of heaven, which is the real treasure for which we all should be striving.

When a lottery prize reaches 100 million or more, tickets are bought by the hundreds every minute. Most buyers have a plan as to what they would do if they won that amount of money. Most say they would spend it on material things. The sad part of this excitement about winning is the stories we hear about previous lottery winners of large sums of money. Most of them probably wish they had never won, since they have told many negative stories about their experiences.

Some people view material things as a status symbol. It makes them feel superior to others who do not have what they have.

Is the possession of material things really worth it in the long run?

We read in the Bible: "What does it profit a man if he were to gain the whole world and lose his soul?

CHAPTER SIX

Prayer and Good Works

The more time that we spend thinking of heaven should help us turn our thoughts to God and then to prayer and good works. Prayer is a form of talking to God. If we talk to Him regularly, it can make a big difference in our lives. We can talk to God any time and any place. We don't have to be in a church or a holy place to do this. If we happen to wake up during the night, we could talk to God; then we would have Him all to ourselves— or maybe not quite! Talking to God often may help us to rethink our priorities in life and then to act on them.

During baseball season we see a number of major league players bless themselves at home plate as they get ready to bat, and after getting a crucial hit or home run, they point to the heavens. This would lead many spectators at the ballpark, as well as television viewers, to recognize that these players are demonstrating a belief in God's intervention and are not afraid to show it.

Knowing how little leaguers and others in youth baseball try to imitate what they see major leaguers do, we shouldn't be surprised to find this sort of thing being done by the younger players. Hopefully, it might cause some of them to become more aware of God's presence on and off the field.

It would be impossible to know how many people are praying for their team to win the game, no matter what the sporting event might be. God cannot answer all their prayers because only one team will win, but at least they are praying and that is the important thing.

Of course, not everyone watching a game is praying; in fact, the likelihood would undoubtedly be very small. Some spectators act in a disgraceful manner, particularly if they have had too much to drink. Hopefully, the prayers that are being said will bring God's blessing on the event so the devil can't claim a victory.

Jesus Himself taught us to pray as we find in Matthew 6: 9-15.

Jesus said: *"Pray then in this way: Our Father in Heaven, hallowed be your name. Your kingdom come, Your will be done, on earth as it is in heaven. Give us this day our daily bread and forgive us our debts, as we also have forgiven our debtors. And do not bring us to the time of trial, but rescue us from the evil one. For if you forgive others their trespasses, your heavenly Father will also forgive you, but if you do not forgive others, neither will your Father forgive your trespasses.* The wording has changed over the years!

In Matthew 7:7-8, we find:

"Ask, and it will be given you; search, and you will find; knock, and the door will be opened for you. For everyone who asks receives, and everyone who searches finds, and for everyone who knocks, the door will be opened."

Again we find in Matthew 21:22:

"Whatever you ask for in prayer with faith, you will receive."

In Mark Gospel 11:24 we hear Jesus saying:

"So I tell you, whatever you ask for in prayer, believe that you have received it, and it will be yours."

In Jeremiah 29:12:

"Then when you call upon me and come and pray to me, I will hear you."

We find in Colossians 4:2:

"Devote yourselves to prayer, keeping alert in it with thanksgiving.

In Phillippians 4:6-7:

"Don't worry about anything; instead, pray about everything.
"Tell God what you need, and thank him for all he has done. If you do this, you will experience God's peace, which is far more wonderful than the human mind can understand."

In 1 Thessalonians 5:17

"Keep on praying."

Catholics believe that praying to the saints is a means of them interceding to God for us. They also pray directly to God, especially when they say the Our Father and as they follow prayers said at Mass by the priest.

Some Catholics have a particular saint to whom they have a special devotion. Of course, Mary, the mother of Jesus, is no doubt the most popular and best loved saint. Catholics, by untold numbers, say the rosary every day or at least regularly.

The lives of saints have been written about in numerous religious books and publications. Although their stories are extremely interesting, for the most part most Catholics are not knowledgeable about them.

Imagine meeting the saints when we arrive in heaven! If we had a special devotion to one in particular and had prayed to him or her often, what a reunion that would be!

People of other religions downplay the spiritual devotion that Catholics show to saints. Some even feel their veneration borders on idolatry. It is true there may be some devout Catholics who demonstrate their love for a particular saint beyond the norm, but if they were asked, they probably would not say they idolize the saint.

Is praying to the saints an effective way of getting our prayers answered? In heaven we will find out for sure, but for now we will continue the practice.

The author of *Go to Heaven* prays to God and to several saints at daily Mass and feels his prayers have been answered in many cases. We all know we cannot have everything we ask for.

Even if we feel our prayers are never answered, don't give up; be persistent. In heaven, we will discover how our prayers were handled. Can you imagine how many prayers storm heaven every minute of the day and night!

We should remember that prayer is good for the soul and that God hears our prayers, even if He is not always ready to grant our requests at the time we make them.

Readers may or may not be aware of The National Day of Prayer, which is held on the first Thursday of May each year. On this day thousands of events are conducted throughout the country and many volunteers are needed to make it successful. These observances are held in government buildings, schools, businesses, churches and homes. Much more information can be found on their website, which is www.nationaldayofprayer.org.

What kind of good works could we do? Well, we could decide to do less for ourselves and more for others. We could think about volunteering our services in some capacity. We could visit someone in a nursing home—someone who never has any visitors. Imagine how much comfort that would be for a person who could be very lonely. There are many opportunities for us to be volunteers right in our own hometowns.

We might consider how we treat other people, including our own family members. We could show more thoughtfulness to those with whom we come in daily contact. A kind act can go a long way!

Doing good works certainly puts us on the right path to heaven if our motives are sincere.

We find the Golden Rule in Matthew 7:12:

> "In everything do to others as you would have them do to you;
> for this is the law and the prophets."

Again in Matthew 16:27:

"When He comes, He will repay each man according to his conduct."

And in Jeremiah 17:10:

> "I, the Lord, alone probe the mind and test the heart, to reward
> everyone to the merit of his deeds."

And in Revelation 20:12:

> "…lastly, among the scrolls, the book of the living was opened.
> The dead were judged according to their conduct as recorded on the
> scrolls."

A good deed could be as little an act as opening a door for someone to let that person go through ahead of us.

We could plan to do good things by making a list of what we might want to do for others until this becomes an established habit. The less we think of satisfying our own needs, the more we can reflect on helping others, especially those in need.

Once prayer and good works are an established part of our lives, we can devote time to try to get others to do likewise. Often when we are motivated to do things, we feel the urgency to have others join forces with us. This sort of thing happens when someone, who gave up smoking after many years, now wants his friends who smoke to abstain as well.

Setting a good example for others by the way we live can certainly influence others to follow suit. Have we not said to ourselves, at one time or another, how we wish we could be more like someone whose behavior we held in high esteem?

We often find ourselves looking for role models, especially for our children. It is our hope that someone who is in the limelight, such as a public servant or an athlete, might be a good influence on those who admire them. Unfortunately, we are often disappointed when we read negative stories about famous people who are greatly admired.

Fortunately, in our midst, we have people whom we do not read about or see on television, but who are truly unsung heroes and role models for us all. They would be found in all walks of life, such as teachers, policemen, firemen, doctors, fathers, mothers, husbands, wives, uncles, aunts, grandfathers, and grandmothers just to list a few. Much of what these people do for us may go unnoticed or unappreciated.

What we should do is try to notice the good that others are doing and praise them accordingly. A compliment can go a long way. We should make it a point to offer compliments as often as possible. Often saying "thank you" is a nice gesture.

If we admire what people do for others, we should, in turn, try to emulate what they do. Helping others, particularly the unfortunate and helpless, is a very rewarding experience.

The author of this book compares life to a football or basketball game in which there are four quarters. The first quarter would be from ages 0-25; the second would be from ages 26-50; the third 51-75 and the fourth 76-100. Beyond 100 would be overtime. It is truly amazing how quickly these quarters in life go by.

What we need to do to prepare for heaven is a game plan—a well thought out plan of action. This plan should set goals for the day, the week , the month and the year. Goals should not be difficult to reach but something we can easily manage.

What kind of goals do we want to achieve? They should mainly be goals that enrich our lives and those of others and also set us on the right path toward our eternal reward in heaven. These goals can differ from person to person in the manner in which they are established.

We might decide to do one kind deed for somebody each day for a week. It can be for the same person or several different ones. It may be something we have planned or something we do on the spur of the moment. The important thing is to carry out what we have decided to do. This is how we form good habits and establish commitment in our lives.

Another goal could be to eradicate one of our bad habits. We all have habits that need to be changed from bad to good. Choose one and for a week make some adjustment to it. During the following week make another adjustment. Before we may even realize it, we may find someone noticing this change in us. That will add to our motivation and keep us committed. Forming good habits and changing bad ones both require dedication on our parts. We need to devise a plan and stick to it.

If we focus on this aspect of our lives, we can make a difference in the way we feel and in how we can make an effect on others.

If we admire what people do for others, we should in turn try to emulate what they do. There is no reason why we could not aspire to be role models for those with whom we come in contact, particularly the young people in our lives.

CHAPTER SEVEN

Church Closings

Those Catholics who have had their churches closed have been hurt, angered, disappointed, disgusted and saddened by this whole ordeal, and there is no reason why they shouldn't have these feelings. This is a most difficult situation for them and a tremendous loss for them to experience.

Some of them have threatened to leave the church; others say they would not contribute any more. This is a sad time for victims of church closures. It will take a long time for many of them to recover from this experience of loss and deprivation. Unfortunately, some will never again regain the spirit they once enjoyed.

Their church meant so much to them in so many ways. Many were baptized, confirmed and married in these churches, as well as their children and grandchildren, in some cases.

So many of these Catholics are still reeling from the effects of the priest abuse scandal, and then to have their place of worship removed has to be heart-wrenching.

Some of these Catholics will immediately move to a nearby parish, will find they are certainly welcomed there and will go on with their Christian lives. Others will gradually make the transfer to another church and eventually will fit right in, even though it may take as long as a year or two for this to happen. But some, and it may be many, will harbor such feelings of anger and distrust that it will take a very long time for them to heal. Some may stop going to church altogether.

What these Catholics must realize is God knows the pain and mental suffering they are enduring over all of this. Even God cannot prevent the closing of churches, but He can certainly help ease the pain if He is prayed to and asked for help. He is our source of comfort whenever we are feeling down and out.

Heaven is our goal and no matter what happens in our short lives on earth, no matter what losses we suffer, we must keep our minds on the grand prize of all—heaven.

CHAPTER EIGHT

Our Guardian Angels

Many people with little or no faith give no thought to their guardian angels. It might even be true that many who have faith seldom think of them. In fact, it requires faith to believe that we have guardian angels.

Suppose our guardian angel is one of our deceased loved ones; a parent, a sibling or a close relative. We have no way of proving or disproving such a thing. If this were true, would we give more thought to what we do and how we act on a daily basis?

We could even pretend that our guardian angel is a loved one who has died and could converse with him or her as we go about our daily lives. Our real guardian angel certainly would not mind this case of mistaken identity.

Before we make any important decisions, we could ask our guardian angel for advice. We may not realize his or her input, but it is possible that it was given.

If some people have very bad habits, they might think twice before doing them if they felt their guardian angel, who might be their mother, is watching over them.

Even if our guardian angel is not a deceased relative of ours, having one as a companion can keep us from ever feeling lonely or unwanted.

Often reciting the common prayer to our guardian angel can help us focus on his or her presence. In case you have not heard it or have forgotten it; it is on the next page.

Angel of God, my guardian dear, to whom His love commits me here, ever this day/night be at my side, to light and guard, to rule and guide. Amen.

This prayer can be said any place, any time, day or night and as often as we wish. Just before retiring for the night would be an excellent time to say it.

This author remembers reading an article in the *Boston Globe* about a man who, while playing bocce with his friends, suffered a heart attack and collapsed. His friends, not knowing what to do as his face turned blue, tried to revive him by pounding on his chest but to no avail.

Suddenly out of nowhere, a bicyclist stopped, performed CPR until firefighters arrived, and then rode off without mentioning his name to anyone.

When the victim arrived at the hospital, the attending physician said the bicyclist's efforts prevented brain damage and cardiac arrest.

The man insisted his life was saved by an angel sent by Saint Anthony, for whom he has great devotion.

There have been many attempts to find out who this bicyclist was. It could very well be a case of just a good Samaritan being at the right place at the right time, or could it have been a guardian angel sent by God?

Your author recalls a time when he was serving in the armed forces. He was driving along the side of a mountain road in the Rocky Mountains of New Mexico. He foolishly passed another car on a curve and just after doing that he noticed an eighteen-wheel truck coming in the opposite direction. If the truck had been there a few seconds earlier, it would have pushed your author's vehicle, which had two passengers in it, over the mountain side, and no doubt the truck would have gone over as well.

This potential disaster taught your author a lesson he never forgot, even though it happened nearly sixty years ago. He could have met his Creator that day, but someone was watching over him. Was it his guardian angel? He will find out someday for sure!

More recently, while traveling with his wife, her sister and husband along a road in Virginia, your author observed a car weaving out of control going in the opposite direction. In a matter of seconds, this other vehicle flew airborne right across the divided highway heading toward our car.

Anticipating a disaster in the making, your author pressed the gas pedal to the floor and avoided a horrific collision. Three girls in the other vehicle landed upside down in an adjacent field. Miraculously, none of them was injured.

Were our guardian angels watching over us that day? It was either that or we were all very lucky!

How many people could cite similar stories that were near-misses or potential disasters!

Examples, such as those your author gave, could be told by untold numbers of people throughout history. When we get to heaven, we will meet whoever had been our guardian angel. There will be a lot to talk about regarding the role he or she played in our lives.

If we communicate with our guardian angel now and show our appreciation, he or she might just give us that extra bit of attention that could make the path to heaven that much smoother.

CHAPTER NINE

Hour of Our Death

What if we knew the exact day and hour that we were to die? What would we do differently as that day and hour drew near? How would we prepare for it?

Some people might charge their credit cards up to the maximum and escape to a faraway, exotic island somewhere. Other people might go to a church or synagogue and quietly pray for forgiveness of their past sins. What would you do?

Realistically, we should live our lives in such a way that we will always be prepared to depart from this world and enter the next, but that is not reality for the majority of people.

Most people give very little thought to when they might die. They are too distracted by what is going on in their lives, even though they know they will die sometime. Older people certainly think about it more often, especially as they see their aged friends and relatives pass away one by one. Young people are more apt to think about death when a tragic accident claims a friend or family member.

None of us really know when we will die, so it is important to always be prepared. This is not easy to do. It takes a long time to condition ourselves to focus on leaving this world with so many things going on all the time.

For example, when we are driving our cars, we need to pay attention to the rules of the road, where we are going and how others are driving near us. Dying is not even on our minds, yet many thousands die every year in automobile accidents.

At the workplace, there are so many things going on that death is only discussed if a fellow worker has lost a close friend or family member.

A marriage ceremony is one of the happiest occasions that we may witness, and yet we hear the words "until death do us part." Unfortunately, fifty percent of marriages part long before death.

We hear about people dying all the time when we watch the news on television or when we read the newspaper. It might be an earthquake, a hurricane, a tornado, a forest fire, a terrorist attack, a murder, etc. Whatever the cause, we hear and read about death on a daily basis.

If someone close to us dies, we experience a much greater loss than if we hear about the death of someone we don't know. Even if we read about some tragedy in which many people die, we feel a degree of sorrow for them, but we soon forget about the occurrence. The loss of a loved one, however, may linger in our hearts and minds for a long, long time.

So as common as death is to us, not many dwell on their own demise. Since we have no idea when we'll die or where, we just don't spend a lot of time thinking about it.

Many Catholic Christians say the Hail Mary frequently, and at the end of this prayer, they say the words: "Holy Mary, mother of God, pray for us sinners, now, and at the hour of our death. Amen." If they recite the rosary, they would be repeating this over fifty times.

There is no reason why all Christians and non-Christians alike should feel excluded from saying the Hail Mary. The entire prayer is as follows:

Hail Mary, full of grace, the Lord is with thee. Blessed art thou amongst women and blessed is the fruit of thy womb, Jesus. Holy Mary, mother of God, pray for us sinners, now, and at the hour of our death. Amen.

A prayer this author often recites goes as follows:

Jesus, Mary and Joseph, I give you my heart and my soul.
Jesus, Mary and Joseph, assist me in my last agony.
Jesus, Mary and Joseph, may I breathe forth my soul in peace with you. Amen.

There are many other prayers that can be said whether they are formal or informal. The main thing is that you talk to God in any format you choose.

CHAPTER TEN

Last Judgment Day

It is difficult to envision what the Last Judgment Day will be like. There has never been one, so how could we possibly know? We do get insights from passages in the Bible and these will be cited later in this chapter.

Imagine assembling all the people whoever lived plus all those who have not been born yet! The sheer numbers are impossible to comprehend. When we see pictures on television of huge throngs of people gathered for some important event, we might find that amazing. We would have to multiply that number of people by a number that is too large to imagine in order to determine how many of us will appear at the Last Judgment. We can be certain that our loving God will handle this situation as only He could.

If there will only be two places for us to go, heaven or hell, our choice naturally would be heaven. Unfortunately, we will not be making the choice at that time. How we conducted our lives and the choices we made while on earth will determine what our destination will be.

Just picture the scene at the Last Judgment Day! The Bible mentions much "weeping and gnashing of teeth." Imagine loved ones being separated for all eternity!

Temporary separations that we experience on earth can be very stressful, especially if there is a threat of danger like going off to war. Permanent separations, as we experience when a loved one dies, can cause much sadness, but at least we know we will be together with the deceased after our lives end. The unanswered question is, will we?

Suppose we are all gathered together at the Last Judgment at which time we will be told where we will spend all eternity and you notice your son being given the signal that he will be going to hell. He turns to you and says:

"Why didn't you persuade me to lead a better life on earth. I don't want to burn in hell forever. Couldn't you have done more for me when you had the chance? You knew it was going to be like this, didn't you? This means I'll never see you or Mom ever again, doesn't it?"

You might turn to him and say:

"Son, we tried to get you to think more about God and heaven, but maybe we didn't try hard enough. We prayed for you every day; perhaps we should have prayed more than we did. This causes us much pain to see you in this desperate state."

That scenario will be played over and over again as loved ones, family members, lifelong friends, coworkers, teammates, etc., will feel the pain of total separation for all eternity.

Many of us have experienced the feeling of loneliness when someone we deeply love has been taken away from us, either by death, going off to war or for some other reason. It is impossible to imagine what feelings we will have at the Last Judgment Day when we see loved ones leave us for all eternity. What a sad moment it will be for those destined for hell!

If only we could have a dress rehearsal to actually find out who is going where at the Last Judgment. Many people would change their lifestyles in a hurry if they knew hell was going to be their future home. Unfortunately, there will be no such rehearsal.

If people are going to change their evil ways, they need to do it while they are still on earth. He who hesitates is lost, as the saying goes.

If we had chosen to exclude God from our lives during our tenure on earth, then it does not seem likely that He will include us to spend eternity with Him.

If we believe in God, we need to prove our faith in Him. Our faith should include our love of God and to prove that, we need to keep His commandments.

We might wonder who will be sent to hell for all eternity. What kind of behavior will cause anyone to go there? We know there are evil people in our world. We read and hear about people who do terrible things, but as bad as someone is during life, that person could ask God for forgiveness at the time of death and gain eternal life because our All Loving God is also All Merciful.

36

The following list could very well include those people who will be going to hell for all eternity:

> Movie makers who show extreme violence, death and destruction for the sole purpose of making money at the expense of impressionable youth.
> Drug dealers who are responsible for young people becoming addicted and corrupted.
> Pimps who force young girls into prostitution and physically abuse them.
> Those who abuse others, especially very young children, sexually, physically and emotionally.
> Those who steal from others, whether it a large corporation or a small company.
> Those who kill and murder.

Consider this scenario at the Last Judgment Day.

How will pro-choice advocates, who believe in abortion, justify themselves before their Creator? The Fifth Commandment says "Thou shall not kill." Do they believe that babies are not killed by means of abortion? Are they convinced that life does not exist until the actual birth of a baby? How will God question them about this whole matter?

What will those priests who sexually abused children say to God on that last day? For that matter, what will anyone whoever abused another, whether physically, sexually or emotionally, say to God when they meet Him for the first time?

How will "swingers" and others who believe in swapping spouses answer to God on that final day?

What will those who turned away from God while on earth say to Him? Will they have valid reasons? Was it because they encountered an uncaring pastor, a church closing, a church law they disagreed with or some other reasons?

Lists such as this could go on endlessly, but unfortunately there will be many who will suffer in hell for all eternity. The numbers may well be in the millions, maybe even billions. We won't know until Judgment Day.

Can some of these people who are slated for hell be saved? Of course, but they must repent for their sins. Should we pray for them? Positively—since we know how powerful prayer is as you have read in chapter six.

We do not yet know with certainty who will suffer in hell, and we definitely hope and pray that it will not be us or any of our loved ones.

The Bible does give us some indication of who will be going to hell. We find in Revelations 21:8:

> "But as for the cowardly, the faithless, the polluted, the murderers, the fornicators, the sorcerers, the idolators, and all liars, their place will be in the lake that burns with fire and sulfur, which is the second death."

As for appearing at the Last Judgment, we find in Corinthians 5:10:

> "For all of us must appear before the judgment seat of Christ, so that each may receive recompense for what has been done in the body, whether good or evil."

Two other passages your author highly recommends are in Matthew 25: 31-46 and 2 Thessalonians 1: 5-12. You should read these before going on to the next chapter.

Should we all be preparing for this Last Judgment Day? We should be, but are we? What can we do? Could reading this chapter or even the entire book make a difference in anyone's life? Your author certainly hopes so! Would reflecting on what it may be like on the Last Judgment Day make anyone change? Can we prevent anyone from going to hell? There are so many questions. Where do we start? Do we preach to them? Are we confident ourselves about being prepared for the Last Judgment?

What we need to focus on is how to direct our lives toward reaching our goal, which is heaven. There are suggestions in this book that will assist readers to reach that goal. Share this book with as many friends, relatives and family members as you possibly can. They may find inspiration in the book that might head them in the right direction toward heaven.

If we can make heaven a priority by discussing it more often with our loved ones and our friends, who knows—this could even be enough to make a difference in how they live their lives! Making frequent references to heaven in our daily conversation could very easily get our listeners to reflect on heaven, even if it is just for a moment. We could ask others, even total strangers, what their feelings are about heaven and what they think heaven will be like. There will be more on this in chapters fifteen and sixteen.

Imagine how we would feel on the Last Judgment Day if we found out we were responsible for causing someone to gain heaven through our intervention!

CHAPTER ELEVEN

Quotations from the Bible on Heaven

There is much written in the Bible regarding eternal life in heaven. Anyone reading *Go to Heaven* is encouraged to read the Bible regularly and to look especially for quotations about heaven that Jesus said. Reading the Bible often can make a big difference in one's life since it brings us closer to God.

One quotation from the Bible that is often displayed on a banner at nationally televised sporting events is from John 3:16:

> "God so loved the world that He gave His only Son that whoever believes in Him may not die but may have eternal life."

Believing in God may be all that is needed to gain heaven, as many believe, but that seems a little too easy for some of us who think we need to do more than just that.

There are many other Bible quotations that have to do with gaining Heaven, such as the following:

Matthew 7:21:
> "None of those who cry out 'Lord, Lord,' will enter the kingdom of God but only the one who does the will of my Father in heaven."

Matthew 19:24:

"…it is easier for a camel to pass through a needle's eye than for a rich man to enter the kingdom of God."

Luke 13:23-24:

"Lord, are there few in number who are to be saved?" He replied: "Try to come in through the narrow door. Many, I tell you, will try to enter and be unable."

Mark 10: 14-15:

"Let the children come to me; do not stop them; for it is such as these that the kingdom of God belongs. Truly I tell you, whoever does not receive the kingdom of God as a little child will never enter it."

Galatians 5:19-21:

"It is obvious what proceeds from the flesh: lewd conduct, impurity, licentiousness, idolatry, sorcery, hostilities, bickering, jealousy, outbursts of rage, selfish rivalries, dissensions, factions, envy, drunkenness, orgies and the like. I warn you, those who do such things will not inherit the kingdom of God."

In the Bible Jesus taught in parables and in Matthew 13:36-53 we find Jesus using parables to explain about heaven and hell. In Matthew 13:10-15 Jesus explains to his disciples why He spoke in parables.

The author of *Go to Heaven* encourages readers to read chapter 13 in Matthew, especially after reading this particular chapter in the book. Throughout the book you will find him recommending that you read certain passages. You may find this a good way to get in the habit of reading the Bible.

CHAPTER TWELVE

Establishing a Closer Relationship with God

One of the biggest problems in the world today is that many people never get close to God. They do not give much, if any, thought to the fact that after they die God will decide where they will spend all eternity.

At the Last Judgment Day it will be too late to wish that they had made more time for God. It is never too late for anyone while here on earth to devote some time every day to God. People make time to do the things they want to do, especially if it gives them pleasure or they have an ulterior motive.

Establishing a closeness to God is not difficult to do. Just reflecting on our Divine Creator for a few minutes every day could be a great way to start developing a nearness to Him. Reading from the Bible every day for a few minutes could be the spark to ignite a greater love for the Lord.

Recite the Our Father, a prayer that Jesus taught us to say. We find that in the Bible. Just plain talking to God, as if He were right next to us, is an excellent way of establishing a loving relationship with God.

None of these suggestions need to take up a lot of time, but they can have long-lasting effects.

Imagine how better we will feel on that day when we will face God Himself knowing we did our best trying to get close to Him while on earth!

CHAPTER THIRTEEN

Free Will

Since God gave us a free will, we can live our lives any way we wish. However, the choice is solely ours to make.

Some people choose to do only those things that give them pleasure, disregarding the feelings of others close to them. The pleasures they seek may be immoral activities, cheating for their own gainful purposes, gambling money that should be going to their households for everyday living expenses, drinking so much that it causes serious hardships for their families, lying to the point where it becomes a way of life, etc.

All of the above can cause untold misery for their loved ones and often these wrongful actions become uncontrollable. Fortunately, help can be provided for those who seek it.

The use of drugs is another pleasure-seeking habit in which people of all backgrounds might indulge. It is such a costly habit that people steal, lie and even commit murder in order to support it.

Can these people gain heaven? Of course, but they will need to change their ways. Is God in their lives? Probably not at the time they are digressing, but He is standing by waiting for them to turn to Him. Many people have done terrible things in their lives and, through the grace of God, they have repented and discovered how wonderful life can be.

The problem is that while they are involved in their sinful ways, they are blinded by their actions and may not even realize the harm and misery they may be causing others, particularly those nearest and dearest to them.

They may not even know that others, especially family members and relatives, are praying for them. At times, it may seem that these prayers are not being answered, but don't give up. The Lord is listening. It may take many years and a lot of prayers before success comes about. We must remember prayer is powerful, as you have read in chapter six.

There are things that can be done to help people change their sinful ways and evil habits. Family members and relatives can talk to those who need help to make them aware of the damage they are doing to everyone including themselves.

Joining Alcohol or Gambling Anonymous has helped thousands of people over the years to turn themselves around and rid them of the demons that have caused havoc in their lives.

Drug addicts also have agencies that offer assistance to meet their needs.

Even though these people made choices to go astray, they can also choose to clean up their bad habits and go on to live normal lives. They may need outside help for this to happen, but a lot depends on their willingness to cooperate in order to make the change.

Hopefully, God will become more a part of their lives and their salvation will not be in jeopardy.

CHAPTER FOURTEEN

Saving Our Youth

In the world that we live in today with so many television shows, movies and music so rampant with sexual overtones and horrific violence as well as the internet with its access to pornography, it is no wonder that many of our youth are so susceptible to active sexual lives, drugs and excessive drinking.

So many children and adolescents are home alone with no supervision while their parents are at work. They are able to watch whatever television programs they wish as well as search online for pornography and chat rooms that are completely unsuitable and harmful to them.

People who produce these television shows and films that are so sexually explicit and/or violent will have to answer to God some day for the evil they have generated and the innocent minds they have corrupted.

The monetary gains they make on earth will be worth nothing on the Last Judgment Day. What do you think God will say to them? Are these people aware of the harm they do to our young people, or are they blinded by the millions of dollars they are making by producing these shows?

To a certain extent, parents can monitor what their children watch on T.V. and how they use the computer by having safeguards installed. Watching selected shows with your children can be a very productive and enjoyable experience for all concerned. Some parents only allow T.V. to be on at certain times and only selected programs to be watched. Some do not permit children to have T.V.s and computers in their bedrooms which, of course, makes monitoring that much more difficult.

It is not easy for parents to install in their children the importance of avoiding situations that are harmful to them. Parents have a big responsibility in raising children, but children, in turn, need to be cooperative on their part.

Talking to your children about what they need to know as they grow and develop is so important. This needs to start in the early years when children are very young, and it needs to be continued on an ongoing basis. Beginning these talks with teenagers could be much too late.

Furthermore, parents need to show by good example in order for children to have proper models to follow. If cursing is used regularly at home, children will pick this up very quickly. When teenagers see their parents doing a lot of drinking and/or using drugs, it sends them a message that it must be alright for them to do such things. Children and adolescents are particularly good listeners when parents are talking to other people on the telephone or elsewhere. They may hear any number of conversations that are not exemplary.

What is the role of children and adolescents in all of this? In this day and age it is not easy growing up from childhood to adulthood. There are many obstacles in the way! Some school-age children may be under much parental pressure to excel in school while others get very little support from home. Teenagers may have to deal with a lot of peer pressure to go along with schoolmates who want them to do things contrary to what their parents have tried to teach them.

Latchkey children can be subjected to all kinds of temptations while being home alone without parental supervision. There are numerous television shows that children should not be watching. Some of the music lyrics that teenagers listen to are filled with words and messages that would make many parents cringe in disbelief if they heard them.

It is no wonder that there is so much sexual activity among teenagers because of the movies, magazines, music and television shows that just bombard them with sensual pictures and words.

Another disturbing factor that young people face today is the possibility of going to war someday if our country continues to be threatened by terrorists. Not only do they hear about the service men and women who are being killed, but they may see older siblings and friends returning from the war in Iraq with missing arms and/or legs and others who are having a great deal of difficulty adjusting to civilian life. This no doubt is very troubling to our young people.

Is there an answer for all this? There is and it means parents and children need more of God in their lives. Some families never go to church or synagogue. Your author devotes chapter four in *Go to Heaven* to reasons why some people don't attend church services and why they should.

46

Getting to know God better by going to church regularly can make a tremendous difference in how we live our lives. It gives us a better outlook on life and helps us to realize why we are on this earth. As we get closer to God we experience a desire to want to be with Him for all eternity. That is why we were born; not for the pleasures that people search for on earth, but to be with our All Loving God forever and ever.

If our young people could only get to know God better by regularly attending church, they would recognize what is truly worthwhile and not be pulled into a world that could turn them away from God.

Parents would find that a closer relationship with God would make raising a family a much more enjoyable undertaking. A family that has God in their lives is a happier family.

CHAPTER FIFTEEN

Evangelizing Heaven Publicly

When this author sees crowds of people gathered together, it makes him wonder how many of them will actually go to heaven. His sense is that the people in the crowd have their minds set on what it is they are doing at that time. They may be watching a sporting event, milling about in a shopping mall, caught in a traffic jam or just being someplace where there happens to be a lot of people. It is safe to say that very few, if any, are thinking about heaven when they are in the company of so many others.

Well then, just when do people think of heaven? Probably, most people only think of heaven when someone in their midst talks about it. If you were to ask people if they plan to go to heaven, most would likely say they would.

The author of *Go to Heaven* wants people to think about heaven more often; every day would be nice! How could this ever become a reality? One solution would be for readers to organize an event or participate in one on The National Day of Prayer services, which are held on the first Thursday of May every year. This would provide those present an opportunity to spend some time reflecting on heaven as part of the observance. Incidentally, readers may wish to go back to chapter six and re-read the information on The National Day of Prayer.

Are there other ways of getting people to dwell on heaven? The book you are now reading is one solution to all of this, but we are talking about millions of people whom the author would like to reach.

Billboard or television advertising about heaven would be too costly and therefore out of the question. If we could get readers of *Go to Heaven* to put ads in their local newspapers, we could reach many people that way. A simple ad could be "Have you thought about heaven lately? Are you taking steps to

48

get there?" The person submitting the ad could include his or her name or just put it through anonymously.

Another method of submitting this to the local paper would be a letter to the editor. The message could be whatever you want to write about heaven. The overall objective should be to get the readers to think about it. If enough of you were to do this in all parts of the country, imagine how many could be reached! This could be an excellent way of delivering a message about heaven to thousands of readers, thereby heightening their awareness of it.

Other readers of *Go to Heaven* may come up with different ways to spread the word about life after death, and this author would welcome whatever they could do to further the cause. A message about heaven could be put on banners and worn on lapel pins by anyone willing to do this. A vanity license plate with the letters that spell heaven would be another way of getting the word out to the public.

Trying to spread the word about our eternal destiny to as many people as we can will certainly please God who is waiting there for us as well as open the door a little wider for us for doing this.

CHAPTER SIXTEEN

Evangelizing Heaven Privately

Will you be ready to die in God's good graces when the time comes? Are you ready right now to meet your Maker as you read this book? Has reading *Go to Heaven* helped you to realize the importance of being prepared to die?

What is the best way to get ready to meet God face-to-face? There is no best way, but many, many different ways. Some people pray a lot and that should keep them well prepared; others spend a great deal of time helping those in need which, to say the least, is a very noble effort on their part. So prayer and good works have to be the key to open the gates of heaven. In chapter six you read about how important they are.

Not only should we get ourselves prepared for our heavenly journey, but how about helping others do the same? Who needs our help? How can we do this? What is the best approach? When and where do we start?

We can answer these questions in one simple sentence if we live exemplary lives and everyone who comes in contact with us wants to imitate us. Unfortunately, such things just don't happen that easily.

What we are talking about is much more complicated. Setting a good example is a beginning, but it will take much effort to win over some people who give little thought to life after death. There are some individuals who don't even believe there is life after death, but those are the hardcore ones with whom we will try to deal later.

Let us begin with those we believe are good and decent people, but who need a helping hand along the way. They just don't spend any time thinking about heaven and that is where we come in. They may need gentle reminders from time to time and that might be enough to get them headed in the right direction.

What about those who never go to church or temple? How do we approach them about heaven? We should be able to talk to them about heaven without convincing them they need to attend church services. That might happen if we can get them excited enough about heaven and what it has to offer them.

The best approach for us to use when discussing heaven with people is to do it matter-of-factly. We can try questions like: Do you think there is a heaven? What do you think it is like there? Are you planning to go to heaven? Whom would you like to meet in heaven? The responses people will give might be what we would expect, and then again, we may be surprised what some might say. We might even find some individuals who don't believe a heaven exists.

When is a good time to broach the subject of heaven with people? Since it is a topic not usually discussed very often, except in church or temple when a priest, minister or rabbi mentions it, it could also be brought up after dinner at home with the family or when dining at a restaurant with friends. A good time would be when people are in a relaxed mood and the conversation is on the light side.

Inviting friends over to the house for an informal chat about a variety of topics might be a successful way to introduce a discussion about heaven, as well as other important matters. This could lead to a weekly or monthly discussion club, a type of forum that has become very popular, and in which all kinds of topics could be covered, including a discussion of this book, *Go to Heaven*. Internet chat rooms would also be an excellent place to talk about heaven to people anywhere in the country.

If heaven is talked about in various circles and more and more people become involved, it becomes a movement of sorts. This would be an excellent challenge for all of us to try to accomplish. Imagine the reunion in heaven we would have with all those whom we had discussions about heaven during our earthly stay! Some of these people may not have gotten to heaven if it had not been for our intervention.

As far as those who either don't believe there is a heaven or are reluctant to talk about it with us, we can let them know we will pray for them with the hope and belief they will change. Very possibly some of them are reading this book and may begin to realize how serious we are in trying to reach them. We want them in heaven with us.

None of us really know what heaven is going to be like, but the author of *Go to Heaven* has written this book with a firm hope that his readers will earnestly strive to enlist as many people as possible to not only talk about heaven, but to do whatever is necessary to convince them to go there and what to do to get there.

Heaven is our eternal reward. Our All Loving God has plans that our finite minds are not capable of even guessing or imagining what He has in store for us.

We must all live our lives every day in the best way possible so that we are headed on the right path to our heavenly destiny. If we falter, as so often we do, let us get right back on that path and courageously move forward. God will be there waiting for us with open arms whenever He decides it is our time to meet Him.

CHAPTER SEVENTEEN

Preparing for Our First Day in Heaven

Most of us remember certain first days that happened in our lives, depending on our current age and memories. Some may remember their first day of school, their first communion day, their first date, their first visit to a special place, leaving home for the first time, etc.

Can we imagine what the first day in heaven could possibly be like? The hearts we now have on earth would probably not be able to withstand the excitement of it all! Undoubtedly, we will be overwhelmed with happiness and joy to a degree that we never experienced here on earth!

Just picture what it will be like to see God face-to-face for the very first time! What will He say to us? What will we say to Him? Will we say such things as: "Why did I not spend more time on earth praying and doing good works? Why did I not spend more time in church or temple? Why did I so often offend you by my transgressions?" Of course, we can answer these questions now by making changes in our lives and getting closer to God while we still have time. Time is on our side right now, so we should make the most of it.

We could try to live our lives with that image in our minds of that initial meeting with our All Loving God. That could make a big difference in how we conduct ourselves.

If we knew we were going to meet a famous or important person on earth, such as the Pope, a king, the president, etc. we certainly would prepare for that event in every way possible. We would do all in our power to learn as much as we could about that person as well as rehearse the things we would want to say. We, no doubt, would become very nervous about this meeting as we approached the scheduled day and time.

Chances are that most of us won't have to worry about such a thing, but meeting our Creator will take place sometime, and it will not be scheduled. It could be tomorrow; we just have no clue as to when the most important moment of our lives will take place.

We know from experience that proper preparation is the key to just about everything. Teams prepare to meet with their opponents with a great deal of anticipation, debaters spend much time preparing their material, lawyers have to do much research getting ready for a court appearance on behalf of their clients, just to mention a few examples.

Does it not make sense that we should strive to do all in our power to get ready to meet our All Loving God?

Trying to spread the word about our eternal destiny to as many people as we can will certainly please God, who is waiting there for us, as well as open the door a little wider for us for doing this.

BIOGRAPHY

Raymond J. Fell

Raymond Fell is a husband, father and grandfather. He is a graduate of Saint Francis Xavier Mission House in Island Creek, Massachusetts. This was a minor seminary run by the Society of the Divine Word Missionaries. Upon graduation, he attended Saint Mary's Seminary in Techny, Illinois, for a period of eight months.

After serving in the Army for nineteen months as a military policeman and receiving an honorable discharge, Raymond enrolled at Boston College Intown where he graduated with a Bachelor of Science degree in economics. At a later date he received a Masters degree in education from Bridgewater State College in Bridgewater, Massachusetts.

Until his retirement, Raymond worked as a teacher and guidance counselor for more than thirty years with the Hingham School Department in Hingham, Massachusetts.

He has always had a keen interest in what heaven might be like and that has prompted him to write his book *Go to Heaven*. His primary goal in writing this book is to attempt to get his readers to give more thought to life after death, particularly in light of all the things going on in the world today.

Printed in the United States
29303LVS00002B/463-468